FROM SIDE HUSTLE TO MAIN HUSTLE

GROWING YOUR BUSINESS SMARTLY

JOHN DOLLAR

Copyright © 2024
by
John dollar

All rights reserved. No part of this book may be reproduced, stored in a retrieval system, or transmitted in any form or by any means, electronic, mechanical, photocopying, recording, scanning, or otherwise, without the prior written permission of the publisher, except for brief quotations in critical reviews or articles.

Table of Contents

Introduction.. 5

Chapter 1 understanding the concept of side hustle.. 15

1.1 Definition of Side Hustles......................... 19

1.2 Importance of Side Hustles in Career Development.. 23

1.3 Transitioning from Side Hustles to Main Hustle... 29

Chapter 2: Identifying Profitable Side Hustles 35

2.1 Assessing Personal Interests and Skills... 41

2.2 Researching Market Trends...................... 44

2.3 Evaluating Potential Income Streams....... 49

2.4 Balancing Passion and Profitability........... 54

Chapter 3: Building and Growing Your Side Hustle.. 61

3.1 Establishing a Solid Foundation................ 66

3.2 Effective Time Management Strategies.... 71

3.3 Marketing and Branding for Side Hustles. 76

3.4 Leveraging Online Platforms and Networking.. 82

Chapter 4 Navigating Challenges and Risks... 87

4.1 Financial Management in Side Hustles..... 92

4.2 Balancing Side Hustles with Main Job Responsibilities.. 97

4.3 Dealing with Competition and Market

Changes...102

4.4 Legal and Regulatory Considerations.....107

Chapter 5: Transitioning from Side Hustle to Main Hustle...113

5.1 Signs It's Time to Make the Transition....119

5.2 Financial Planning for the Transition.......122

5.3 Communicating with Employers or Clients.... 128

5.4 Scaling Up and Scaling Down Strategies..... 1134

Conclusion...141

Long-term Benefits of Side Hustles to Main Hustle Transition...145

Introduction

Once upon a time in the bustling city of Metropolis, there lived a young woman named Lily. She worked as a marketing assistant as a typical 9 to 5 job, but her true passion lay in the art of creating unique, handmade jewelry. Lily spent her evenings and weekends creating intricate pieces inspired by the beauty of nature and her vivid imagination. Little did she know that her side hustle would soon become the main focus of her life.

Lily's journey began when she attended a local craft fair to showcase her handmade jewelry. The positive response she received from visitors and fellow artisans fueled her desire to turn her side hustle into something more. The seed of ambition was planted and she decided to take the leap.

She began to devote more time to her craft, perfecting her skills and experimenting with different materials. Lily also started an online store to reach a wider audience. The early days were challenging as she juggled her full-time job with the growing demands of her

business. Sleepless nights and relentless effort became her routine, but Lily's passion fueled her determination.

Word of mouth and social media played a vital role in spreading the word about Lily's unique creations. Her distinctive style and attention to detail sets her jewelry apart from the mass-produced accessories that flood the market. As the orders mounted, Lily was faced with a critical decision - to continue balancing, or risk having her side rush her main rush.

One day Lily received a large order from a boutique in the fashion district. The boutique owner discovered Lily's work through social media and was impressed by the craftsmanship. The order was so significant that it made Lily think about the possibilities of turning her passion into a full-time profession. The decision weighed heavily on her mind.

After much thought, Lily decided to take the plunge and quit her 9-5 job to pursue jewelry full-time. It was a bold move filled with uncertainty, but she believed in her craft and the potential for growth. Lily turned a corner of her small apartment into a makeshift studio, complete with workbenches, tools, and shelves full of colorful gems.

The transition was not without problems. Lily faced challenges such as managing finances, managing the administrative side of the business and dealing with the unpredictability of self-employment. However, each setback fueled her determination to succeed. She attended workshops and networking events to improve her business skills and connect with other small business owners.

As Lily poured her energy into her main hustle, the rewards began to unfold. Positive reviews and customer testimonials poured in and her online presence continued to grow. Soon, her jewelry was featured in fashion magazines and worn by local influencers. The boutique, which originally placed a major order, became a regular client and Lily's creations were featured prominently in their shop window.

The turning point came when she invited Lily to show her collection at a prestigious fashion event. The exposure catapulted her into the limelight, attracting the attention of not only local fashion designers, but also boutique owners and potential investors. Lily's journey from a marketing assistant with a side hustle to an acclaimed jewelry designer was now complete.

Looking back, Lily couldn't believe how far she had come. The challenges, sleepless nights and uncertainties were worth it. Her decision to turn her passion into her main hustle not only changed her life, but also inspired others to follow their dreams.

In the heart of Metropolis, Lily jewelry has become a symbol of resilience and creativity. Her story resonated with aspiring entrepreneurs, proving that with dedication and courage, one can go from a side hustle to a thriving main hustle. Lily's journey was a testament to the power of passion and the remarkable possibilities that await those brave enough to follow their dreams.

Going from side hustle to main hustle is a transformative experience that encapsulates the dynamic and evolving landscape of business in today's world. In an era characterized by unprecedented connectivity and technological advancement, individuals are increasingly drawn to the allure of growing their own businesses alongside traditional employment. This paradigm shift from conventional career paths to pursuing side hustles reflects not only economic necessity, but also a desire for autonomy, creativity, and diversification. When we delve into the complexities of this transition, it becomes clear that the path from side hustle to main hustle is paved with challenges, opportunities, and the inner human desire for self-actualization.

The concept of the side hustle has gained remarkable traction in recent years, fueled by the gig economy, digital platforms and the democratization of business. A side hustle is basically an additional income generating activity performed in addition to the main job. It functions as a financial safety net, a creative outlet, or a means to explore entrepreneurial aspirations without the immediate pressure to rely solely on your success. The rise of freelancing, online marketplaces, and the availability of e-commerce have greatly facilitated the emergence and growth of side hustles, creating an environment where individuals can experiment with their ideas and passions.

Deciding to transition from side hustle to main hustle is a pivotal moment that requires careful consideration and strategic planning. What begins as a side effort can develop into a full-fledged business venture, fueled by entrepreneurial determination and market validation. This journey involves navigating the complex interplay of financial stability, risk-taking, and cultivating the skills necessary for sustained success. Many individuals embark on this trajectory guided by a compelling vision, a unique value proposition, or an unshakable belief in their business's potential to meet market needs.

One of the fundamental challenges in transitioning from side hustle to main hustle is balancing the demands of your entrepreneurial endeavors with your existing commitments. Whether juggling a full-time job, academic pursuits, or family responsibilities, entrepreneurs must carefully manage their time and energy to avoid burnout and maintain a semblance of stability. This often requires strategic prioritization, effective time management, and cultivating a resilient mindset capable of navigating the inevitable uncertainties that accompany business.

Major financial considerations come into play in this transition as entrepreneurs face the need to secure sustainable sources of income to replace or exceed their existing income. This requires a rigorous evaluation of the market, pricing strategies and potential funding sources. Entrepreneurs must be adept at financial planning, budgeting and resource allocation to ensure the viability of their main hustle. The financial dimension of this transition is not only a pragmatic necessity, but also a test of an entrepreneur's ability to adapt and thrive in a competitive business environment.

The evolution from side hustle to main hustle is often marked by a paradigm shift in thinking. Entrepreneurs must move from viewing their business as a sideline to fully embracing the responsibilities and challenges of running a sustainable business. This mental shift involves cultivating resilience, adaptability and a long-term vision. The ability to learn from failures, respond to market feedback, and stay tuned to evolving trends is critical to the success of a mainstream hustle.

Market research and a deep understanding of customer needs are essential elements of this journey. Entrepreneurs must refine their value proposition, identify their target audience and differentiate their offering in a crowded market. The success of the main hustle depends on the entrepreneur's ability to not only meet, but also exceed customer expectations, foster loyalty and continuous growth. This iterative process of refinement and adaptation is central to the entrepreneurial journey and distinguishes those who successfully transition from side hustle to main hustle.

The role of mentorship and networking cannot be overstated in this transition. Entrepreneurs greatly benefit from seeking advice from experienced mentors who can provide insights, share lessons learned, and offer a broader perspective on future challenges. Networking within the entrepreneurial ecosystem opens the door to collaboration, partnerships and opportunities that can catalyze the growth of the main hustle. The collective wisdom and support of a network can prove invaluable when navigating the complexities of business.

As the side hustle turns into the main hustle, branding and marketing become key components of business strategy. Entrepreneurs need to create a compelling story about their business, create a strong online presence and use different marketing channels to reach and engage their target audience. Building a brand that resonates with customers is not only a means to drive sales, but also a way to create a lasting and positive impression in the minds of consumers.

The journey from side hustle to main hustle encapsulates the essence of business today, a dynamic, multi-faceted and often challenging business. It requires a confluence of strategic planning, financial acumen, adaptability and resilient thinking. Entrepreneurs who successfully navigate this transition are those who can strike a delicate balance between passion and pragmatism, creativity and strategic thinking. As the business landscape continues to evolve, the trajectory from side hustle to main hustle remains a testament to

the enduring human spirit of innovation and pursuit
of self-actualization.

Chapter 1 understanding the concept of side hustle

In the dynamic environment of today's workforce, the term "side hustle" has come to the fore as individuals seek alternative sources of income and avenues for personal and professional growth. A side business is basically a side job or business done alongside the main job. As people explore their passions, skills and entrepreneurial spirit, many find themselves on the path from a humble side hustle to a full-fledged main hustle. This transformation often involves a mixture of determination, strategic decision-making and adaptability. In this article, we'll delve into the nuances of understanding the concept of side rushes, explore how they evolve into main rushes, and the key factors that contribute to this transition.

1. Genesis of side hustles:

Understanding the roots of the side hustle phenomenon requires recognizing the changing nature of the work and economic landscape. Factors such as the gig economy, technological advances, and the desire for financial autonomy have fueled the rise of side hustles. People now see their skills and passions not just as hobbies, but as potential sources of income. The flexibility that side hustles provide allows individuals to explore a variety of interests without fully committing to one career path.

2: Identifying catalysts for transition:

Many individuals embark on their side hustle with the intention of supplementing their income, testing business ideas, or pursuing a passion project. However, some catalysts often propel a side hustle to become a main hustle. These catalysts may include financial viability, increasing demand for ancillary products or services, or personal realization of untapped potential. Recognizing these catalysts and using them strategically is critical to a successful transition.

3: Navigating Challenges Along the Way:

The journey from side hustle to main hustle is rarely smooth. Entrepreneurs face challenges such as time constraints, financial uncertainty and the need to balance multiple responsibilities. Learning how to deal with these challenges is critical to sustaining and growing a side hustle. This section explores common barriers and offers insights into overcoming them, emphasizing the importance of resilience and adaptability.

4: Building a solid foundation:

As a side hustle gains momentum and turns into a main hustle, entrepreneurs need to focus on building a solid foundation for their business. This includes strategic planning, financial management and developing a robust business model. Effective marketing and networking become essential to reach a wider audience and create a brand presence. At this stage, it is crucial to emphasize the importance of scalability and long-term sustainability.

5: Balancing Passion and Pragmatism:

Evolving from side hustle to main hustle often requires a delicate balance between passion and pragmatism. While the initial motivation may have been driven by personal interests, the transition requires a realistic assessment of market dynamics, competition and financial viability. Entrepreneurs must be willing to adapt their strategies, refine their offerings, and make decisions that align with their passion as well as the practicalities of running a successful business.

Understanding the concept of side hustles and their evolution into main hustles involves recognizing the multifaceted nature of this entrepreneurial journey. From the genesis of side hustles fueled by a changing economic environment to mastering challenges and identifying transition catalysts, individuals must develop adaptability and resilience. Building a solid foundation, mastering challenges, and balancing passion with pragmatism are critical elements to successfully turning a side hustle into a thriving main hustle. Ultimately, this journey is a testament to the entrepreneurial spirit, where the pursuit of personal and financial fulfillment converges into a sustainable and rewarding enterprise.

1.1 Definition of Side Hustles

Side hustles have become ubiquitous in today's dynamic economy and represent a significant shift in the way people approach their careers. A side hustle essentially refers to a side job or project that individuals pursue in addition to their primary source of income. This extra effort is often driven by passion, skill, or a desire to increase financial stability. In this survey, we'll delve into the definition of side hustles, the motivations behind pursuing them, and how some have successfully transformed their side hustles into main hustles and reshaped their career trajectories.

Definition of lateral movements:
By its very nature, side hustles include a diverse range of activities that individuals engage in to supplement their primary income. It could be a freelance gig, a small business, or even a passion project with the potential to generate additional income. What separates a side hustle from a

traditional part-time job is the personal investment and entrepreneurial spirit. Side hustles are often born out of a desire for financial freedom, skill development, or the pursuit of personal interests that transcend the confines of a nine-to-five job.

Motivation behind Side Hustles:

Understanding the motivations that lead individuals to pursue side hustles is essential. Many of them are motivated by the prospect of extra income, especially at a time when financial security is a top priority. The flexibility that a side hustle offers is another key motivator that allows individuals to balance multiple commitments and explore their passions simultaneously. Additionally, the desire for creative expression and personal fulfillment often compels individuals to invest time and effort in activities beyond their primary occupation.

The evolutionary path from secondary to main business:

For some, what starts as a supplemental source of income develops into a full-fledged main hustle that reshapes their career path. The progression from side hustle to mainstream is a testament to the changing nature of work and the opportunities presented by the digital age. As individuals gain confidence, skills, and experience in their side hustles, they often find themselves at a crossroads where a decision must be made to continue in the security of their primary job or make the leap to making their side the main focus of their work. career.

Transition Challenges and Rewards:

Turning a side hustle into a main hustle isn't without challenges. The uncertainty of business, the financial risks and the need for sustained effort can be daunting. However, those who successfully complete these challenges often reap significant rewards. The autonomy and fulfillment that comes with turning a passion project into a sustainable career path can be immensely satisfying. This shift also gives individuals more control over their time and the opportunity to align their work with their values.

Case studies of successful transitions:

Examining real-life case studies is instructive to illustrate the journey from side hustle to main hustle. The stories of entrepreneurs who have turned a part-time passion into a thriving business show the variety of ways and strategies used. These cases not only inspire budding entrepreneurs, but also offer valuable insights into the practical aspects of navigating this transition, from managing finances to building a customer base.

The concept of side hustles has evolved to be more than just a means of generating extra income. It has become a tool for personal and professional growth, allowing individuals to explore their passions, acquire new skills, and ultimately turn those endeavors into a main hustle. The journey from side hustle to main hustle is a testament to the resilience and adaptability of individuals in the face of changing economic conditions. As the gig economy continues to thrive, the story of side hustles transitioning into mainstream hustles will undoubtedly play a key role in shaping the future of work.

1.2 Importance of Side Hustles in Career Development

Going from side hustle to main hustle is a journey that has a lot of significance for career development. In today's dynamic and competitive job market, individuals are increasingly realizing the value of cultivating additional sources of income beyond their primary employment. This recognition led to the rise of the side hustle phenomenon. In this contextual survey, we delve into the multifaceted aspects of side hustles and how they contribute to a broader spectrum of career development, ultimately paving the way for some to turn their passion projects into full-time endeavors.

The emergence of side hustles:
The term "side hustle" refers to any type of job done in addition to a full-time job. These businesses often stem from personal interests, skills or entrepreneurial ambitions. The emergence of side hustles can be attributed to a variety of factors, including the desire for financial stability,

the search for creative outlets, and the changing landscape of traditional employment.

Financial resilience and stability:
One of the main drivers for individuals who get involved in side hustles is the search for financial resilience. The uncertain nature of the job market along with economic fluctuations motivated people to diversify their income streams. A side hustle can serve as a financial safety net that provides an additional source of income that can be critical during times of economic instability or unexpected expenses.

Skill development and entrepreneurial spirit:
Side hustles offer a unique platform for individuals to hone and expand their skills. Whether it's graphic design, content creation, coding or marketing, these businesses often require a diverse range of skills. Engaging in a side hustle can provide a valuable learning experience that allows individuals to gain new competencies that may not be fully utilized in their primary job.

The side hustle also feeds the entrepreneurial spirit. They encourage individuals to take initiative, be resourceful and think creatively to make their business a success. These entrepreneurial qualities are transferable and can significantly increase effectiveness in a primary career.

Networking opportunities;
The world of side hustles often involves connecting with like-minded individuals, freelancers, and entrepreneurs. This extended network can be a gold mine of career opportunities. Whether it's collaborating on projects, prospecting for potential clients, or exploring new career paths, relationships built through side hustles can open doors that might not be accessible in a traditional career.

Passion and job satisfaction:
Side hustles often revolve around personal passions and interests. Engaging in work that aligns with your passions can bring a deep sense of fulfillment and job satisfaction. Pursuing passion projects outside of regular work hours can inject energy and enthusiasm into an individual's overall

professional life. This increased sense of purpose can positively affect performance in the primary job and contribute to long-term career satisfaction.

Transition from Side Hustle to Main Hustle:
As individuals delve into their side hustles, some may begin to consider turning these businesses into their main source of income. This transition is often fueled by a combination of factors, including the growing success of a side hustle, a strong passion for work, and a desire for greater autonomy.

Financial considerations and planning:
Before jumping from your side hustle to your main hustle, careful financial consideration is paramount. Assessing the stability and sustainability of side income is essential. Individuals need to assess their financial preparedness and ensure they have a financial cushion to cope with the potential uncertainties associated with the move.

Building solid foundations:

Successful transitions from side hustles to main hustles often involve laying a solid foundation. This includes formalizing business structures, developing a comprehensive business plan and building a robust online presence. Attention to legal and financial aspects is essential to ensure a smooth and sustainable transition.

Effective transition management:
Transitioning from side hustle to main hustle requires effective time management and strategic planning. Individuals must assess their current commitments, both personal and professional, and develop a transition plan. This may involve gradually reducing the hours of the primary job as the side hustle gains momentum.

Risks and Rewards:
Like any career move, going from side hustle to main hustle comes with risks and rewards. Autonomy and the potential for greater financial gains may be appealing, but they also involve greater levels of responsibility, uncertainty, and the potential for financial instability. Individuals must

carefully consider these factors and be prepared for the challenges that may arise.

The journey from side hustle to main hustle is a transformational process with far-reaching implications for career development. Side hustles play a key role in fostering financial resilience, skill development and entrepreneurial spirit. As individuals explore their passions through these ventures, the possibility of transitioning them into full-fledged careers becomes increasingly viable.

The importance of side hustles in career development lies not only in the diversification of income, but also in the holistic growth and fulfillment they provide. Whether it's expanding your skills, building valuable networks, or pursuing your passion, a side hustle makes a significant contribution to personal and professional development. For those embarking on the journey of turning their side hustle into a main hustle, careful planning, financial considerations, and a strategic approach are necessary to meet the challenges and reap the rewards of this transformational journey.

1.3 Transitioning from Side Hustles to Main Hustle

Making the transition from side hustle to main hustle is a significant and often challenging step on the entrepreneurial journey. Many individuals start their business as a side hustle, testing the waters while maintaining full-time job security. However, as passion and potential collide, the prospect of turning this side hustle into a primary source of income becomes increasingly enticing. This transition requires careful consideration, strategic planning and a willingness to embrace change.

Understanding Side Hustle Dynamics:
Side hustles usually begin as passion projects or creative outlets that allow individuals to explore their interests without the immediate pressure of sustaining their livelihood. They serve as supplemental sources of income, provide financial flexibility and a safety net while doing something

beyond the boundaries of traditional employment. However, as the side hustle gains momentum and proves its viability, the prospect of becoming the main hustle is enticing.

Transition Readiness Assessment:
Before you take the leap, it's important to assess your readiness for the transition. Evaluate the financial stability of your side hustle considering factors such as steady income, market demand, and scalability. In addition, consider your personal readiness emotionally, mentally, and professionally to handle the challenges of running a full time business.

Financial Preparedness and Risk Mitigation:
Financial stability is the cornerstone of a successful transition. Make sure your side hustle consistently generates enough income to cover your basic living expenses. Create a detailed budget that takes into account both personal and business expenses. Build an emergency fund to protect you from potential financial uncertainties during the initial stages of your main hustle.

Risk mitigation is equally important. Diversify your income streams within your main hustle and reduce reliance on a single source. Explore different revenue channels, partnerships or product/service offerings that align with your core business. This strategic approach can help protect against market fluctuations and unexpected challenges.

Building a solid foundation:
A successful main hustle requires a solid foundation. Formalize your business structure, whether you are a sole proprietor, LLC or corporation, based on your business model and long-term goals. Ensure compliance with legal and regulatory requirements to avoid potential setbacks. Invest time in improving your business plan. Clearly articulate your mission, target market, value proposition and growth strategy. A well-defined plan not only serves as a blueprint, but also becomes an essential tool in finding funding or partnerships to scale your core business.

Marketing and Branding Strategies:

Going mainstream requires a more intense focus on marketing and branding. Create a compelling brand story that resonates with your target audience. Invest in professional branding elements such as a visually appealing logo, consistent brand colors and a user-friendly website. Use digital marketing channels to improve your online presence and reach a wider audience.

Consider the power of networks. Attend industry events, reach your target audience on social media, and build relationships with influencers or colleagues in your industry. Effective marketing and branding strategies not only attract customers but also shape your main hustle as a reputable and recognizable brand.

Time Management and Productivity:
Transitioning from side hustle to main hustle often comes with an increased workload. Mastering time management and increasing productivity become paramount. Identify your most productive hours, delegate tasks where possible and prioritize activities that directly contribute to business growth. Implementing effective systems and tools can

streamline processes, allowing you to focus on strategic decision-making and innovation.

Adapting to change and constantly learning:
Entrepreneurship is a dynamic journey marked by constant change. Embrace adaptability as a hallmark of your entrepreneurial spirit. Be prepared to change your strategies, improve your offers and navigate market fluctuations. Constant learning is the key to staying on top of industry trends, new technologies and evolving consumer preferences to stay ahead of the competition.

Looking for mentorship and guidance:
Transitioning to the mainstream can be a daunting task, but you don't have to navigate it alone. Seek mentorship from experienced entrepreneurs who have successfully made a similar transition. Their guidance and insights can prove invaluable, providing you with a plan based on real-world experience. Joining entrepreneurial communities or looking into mentoring programs can connect you with a support network and valuable resources.

Celebrating milestones and staying motivated:
Celebrate milestones along the way as you navigate the challenges of transitioning from side hustle to main hustle. Acknowledge and appreciate the progress you've made, no matter how small. Staying motivated is essential during this transition, and recognizing successes fosters a positive mindset that fuels continued growth.

Moving from side hustle to main hustle is a significant step that requires careful planning, resilience, and a commitment to continuous improvement. By assessing your readiness, ensuring financial stability, building a solid foundation, implementing effective marketing strategies, mastering time management, adapting to change, seeking guidance and celebrating milestones, you can successfully navigate this transition and turn your passion into a thriving side hustle.

Chapter 2: Identifying Profitable Side Hustles

In today's dynamic economic environment, many individuals are looking for opportunities to supplement their income through side hustles. A side hustle is a business done alongside a full-time job, provides additional financial stability, and often serves as a stepping stone to a main hustle. This article explores the process of identifying profitable side hustles and offers insights on how to transition from a side hustle to a full-fledged main hustle.

I. Understanding the Side Hustle landscape

A. Various Side Hustle options

1. Freelance Platforms: Explore popular freelance platforms like Upwork and Fiverr to leverage your skills and earn extra income.

2. E-commerce Ventures: Consider selling handmade crafts or dropshipping products online through platforms like Etsy or Shopify.

3. Digital Marketing Services: Offer your expertise in social media management, content creation or SEO to businesses in need.

4. Consulting: Share your industry knowledge by offering freelance consulting services.

B. Assessment of Personal Interests and Skills

1. Passion Alignment: Identify side issues that align with your passions to ensure long-term motivation and commitment.

2. Leveraging Skills: Use your existing skills or invest time in acquiring new ones to increase your marketability.

II. Profitability Potential Evaluation

A. Market research

1. Target Audience: Understand your potential customers and their needs and tailor your side hustle accordingly.

2. Competitor Analysis: Research competitors to identify market gaps and unique selling propositions for your side.

B. Financial Feasibility

1. Cost Analysis: Calculate the startup costs, ongoing expenses, and potential revenue to determine the financial viability of your side hustle.

2. Streams of Income: Explore different streams of income within your chosen side hustle to maximize your income potential.

III. Managing the transition to the main hustle

A. Setting clear goals

1. Financial Milestones: Set achievable financial goals that signal readiness to transition from side hustle to main.

2. Time Commitment: Define the required level of time commitment to the side hustle and compare it to interim goals.

B. Building a solid foundation

1. Legal Considerations: Ensure compliance with local regulations and tax requirements by registering your side business as a business entity.

2. Financial Planning: Create a comprehensive financial plan to sustain you during the transition phase.

C. Marketing and Branding

1. Brand Development: Create a strong brand identity that differentiates your side hustle in the marketplace.

2. Marketing Strategies: Implement effective marketing strategies to attract larger audiences and increase revenue.

D. Scaling operations

1. Outsourcing: Consider outsourcing tasks with increased hustle and bustle, allowing you to focus on strategic aspects of the business.

2. Technology Integration: Explore technology solutions to streamline operations and increase efficiency.

IV. Overcoming Challenges in Transition

A. Time Management

1. Balancing Priorities: Develop effective time management strategies to handle a full-time job and growing hustle.

2. Transition Phase: Gradually reduce the hours at your main job as the side hustle gains momentum.

B. Financial stability

1. Emergency Fund: Build an emergency fund to help you through financial uncertainties during the transition period.

2. Diversified Income: Explore different sources of income and mitigate the risks of relying solely on a side hustle.

V. Celebrating success and continued growth

A. Recognition of achievements

1. Milestone Celebrations: Recognize and celebrate successes, big and small, to stay motivated.

2. Feedback and Improvement: Collect feedback from customers and colleagues to continuously improve and grow your side hustle.

B. Discovering new classes

1. Diversification: Consider diversifying your offering or entering new markets to sustain growth.

2. Invest in Education: Invest in continuous learning to keep up with industry trends and maintain a competitive edge.

Identifying profitable side problems involves a strategic combination of personal interests, skill assessment, market research and financial planning. Transitioning from side hustle to main hustle requires careful goal setting, building a solid foundation, and overcoming challenges with resilience. By navigating this path thoughtfully, individuals can turn their side hustle into a thriving side hustle, achieve financial independence, and pursue their passions.

2.1 Assessing Personal Interests and Skills

Assessing your personal interests and skills is a critical step in transitioning from side hustle to main hustle. As individuals embark on the journey of turning their passion projects into a primary source of income, understanding their own strengths and preferences becomes paramount.

First, identifying personal interests lays the foundation for a successful shift. What activities spark real enthusiasm? What topics or tasks attract attention even in your free time? The answers to these questions help individuals determine their passions and provide a solid starting point for exploring potential major hustle paths.

At the same time, recognizing your own skills is equally important. Assessing both hard and soft skills, such as technical knowledge, communication and problem-solving abilities, reveals the tools available to build a sustainable core business. This introspection allows for a realistic assessment of the feasibility of transforming a side gig into a full-time job.

Applicants must consider the market demand for their skills and interests. Researching industry trends and identifying market gaps ensures that the chosen major hustle meets current requirements. This strategic approach increases the likelihood of success and mitigates the risks associated with venturing into uncharted territory.

In addition, networking plays a key role in this transition. Connecting with professionals in your chosen field provides insights, mentorship and potential opportunities. Attend industry events, participate in online forums, and seek advice from those who have successfully made the leap from side hustle to major. Learning from the experiences of others can be invaluable in shaping your own path.

Another important aspect is financial readiness. Before making the transition, individuals should assess their financial stability. Creating a realistic budget, understanding potential income fluctuations, and contingency plans for unforeseen challenges are key components to a successful transition. This predictability minimizes financial stress and allows for a smoother transition period.

Developing a strategic plan is essential. Outline short-term and long-term goals and detail the steps needed to achieve them. This plan serves as a guide to help individuals stay focused and organized during the transition. Regularly review and adjust the plan based on progress and changing circumstances.

Continuous learning is the cornerstone of success in any field. Investing time and resources in acquiring new skills or improving existing ones not only increases competence but also improves adaptability. Keeping up with industry advancements positions individuals as valuable assets in the competitive landscape of their chosen major.

Additionally, understanding the legal and regulatory aspects of your chosen field is key. Compliance with industry standards and regulations is non-negotiable for a sustainable main hustle. Seek professional advice where necessary and ensure all legal obligations are met to avoid potential setbacks.

Balancing passion with pragmatism is key. While promoting one's own interests is essential to fulfillment, practical considerations must not be neglected. Assessing the market demand, financial viability and long-term sustainability of the chosen main hustle ensures that the passion is aligned with a realistic business model.

Transitioning from side hustle to main hustle involves a comprehensive assessment of personal interests and skills. By identifying passions, honing skills, understanding market demand, networking, financial planning, setting strategic goals, continuous learning, legal compliance, and maintaining a balance between passion and pragmatism, individuals can navigate this path successfully. Transitioning is not just a job shift, but a holistic transformation that requires careful planning, commitment and resilient thinking.

2.2 Researching Market Trends

In a dynamic business environment, moving from the side hustle to the main hustle requires a thorough understanding of market trends. Researching these trends is not just a strategic move; it is a crucial step to ensure the sustainability and growth of your business. In this survey, we'll dive into the importance of market trend analysis and how it can be the compass that guides your journey from supplemental income to full-fledged business.

Understanding the Side Hustle Phenomenon:
The rise of side hustles has been monumental in recent years. Driven by the desire for financial independence and the pursuit of passion, individuals have turned to side businesses to supplement their primary income. These ventures often begin as experiments that allow individuals to explore their interests without the full commitment of a traditional business.

Shift to Mainstream: A Strategic Move:
For the side hustler, recognizing the right moment to transition into the main hustle is a critical decision. Market trends play a central role in this transition and act as a compass that guides entrepreneurs to sustainable success. Doing thorough research allows you to make informed decisions and mitigate the risks associated with expanding your business.

Discovering the power of market trend analysis

1. Identification of niche opportunities:
Researching market trends reveals opportunities that may be overlooked. Analysis of consumer behavior, preferences and emerging needs can lead to the discovery of untapped markets. As you transition from your side hustle to your main hustle, identifying and catering to these niche markets can be a game changer.

2. Adapting to consumer demands:
Consumer preferences are evolving and it is imperative to remain attuned to these changes. Analyzing market trends will help you understand what consumers are looking for and allow you to tailor your products or services accordingly. This adaptability is essential in turning a side hustle into a sustainable and customer-focused main hustle.

3. Reducing risks and increasing viability:
Understanding market trends is synonymous with risk mitigation. By identifying potential challenges

and opportunities in advance, you can design strategies to effectively navigate uncertainties. This predictability increases the viability of your business and increases the likelihood of a successful transition to mainstream.

Practical steps for researching market trends

1. Use of tools for data analysis:
In the digital age, data is a gold mine. Use analytics tools to gather information about consumer behavior, preferences and industry trends. Platforms like Google Analytics, social media analytics, and market research databases can provide valuable data to help you make decisions.

2. Monitoring competitive strategies:
Competitive analysis is an integral part of market trend research. By observing the strategies of successful competitors, you can identify gaps in the market, assess consumer satisfaction, and refine your own approach. This competitive intelligence is invaluable as you elevate your business to the main stage.

3. Engage your audience:

Directly engaging your target audience is a powerful research tool. Conduct surveys, collect feedback, and actively engage in online communities related to your specialty. This hands-on approach not only provides real-time insights, but also fosters connection with your customer base.

Case Studies: From Side Hustle to Major Success

1. Etsy: Creating a traditional marketplace:

Originally a platform for handmade and vintage items, Etsy is an example of the transition from side hustle to mainstream. Through ongoing analysis of market trends, Etsy has identified a growing demand for unique, personalized products. Today, it stands as a major marketplace connecting artisans with a global audience.

2. Airbnb: Pioneer of the sharing economy:

Airbnb started as a side hustle for its founders, renting out air mattresses in their apartment. Recognizing the trend towards shared consumption and shared accommodation, Airbnb has developed into a major buzz and disrupted hospitality around the world.

The Market Trend Journey:
On the journey from side hustle to main hustle, market trend research is the compass that guides entrepreneurs through uncharted territory. It uncovers opportunities, mitigates risks and ensures your business is aligned with evolving consumer demands. Embrace the power of market trend analysis and let it be the driving force driving your business endeavors to new heights.

2.3 Evaluating Potential Income Streams

In today's dynamic economic environment, the traditional concept of single, stable employment as a primary source of income is evolving. With the rise of the gig economy and entrepreneurial spirit, individuals are increasingly exploring different sources of income, often starting with side hustles. This transition from supplemental source of income to main hustle requires strategic evaluation of potential income streams to ensure sustainable financial success.

Understanding the Side Hustle Phenomenon:
The term "side hustle" has come to the fore as people look for additional sources of income beyond their main job. Side hustles can take many forms, from freelancing and consulting to selling products online or providing services. These endeavors often begin as passion projects or creative outlets, gradually building momentum and generating income. As individuals experience success in their side hustles, the prospect of transitioning to a main hustle becomes a compelling consideration.

Assessing the viability of income streams:
Before jumping from side hustle to main hustle, a comprehensive evaluation of potential income streams is essential. This evaluation includes an examination of current and potential profitability, market demand, scalability, and personal fulfillment associated with each revenue stream.

1. Profitability: Analyzing the financial viability of each revenue stream is paramount. Consider the revenue generated, associated costs and growth potential. A thorough understanding of the financial aspects ensures a sustainable transition.

2. Market Demand: The demand for products or services within a chosen niche determines the success of any revenue stream. Research market trends, competition and customer needs to identify opportunities for growth and sustainability.

3. Scalability:A successful main hustle should be scalable to meet increased workload and demand. Assess whether the chosen revenue stream can be expanded without reducing quality or efficiency.

4. Personal Fulfillment: While financial considerations are essential, personal satisfaction and fulfillment are equally important. A main hustle that aligns with one's passion and skill set is more likely to stick and bring long-term satisfaction.

Balancing risk and stability:

Going from side hustle to main hustle comes with its own level of risk. While side hustles often provide a safety net during experimentation, relying solely on them for income requires careful risk management. Diversifying income streams can mitigate risk and offer stability during fluctuations in any particular market or industry.

Building solid foundations:

Establishing a master hustle requires a solid foundation based on strategic planning and realistic goals. Develop a comprehensive business plan that outlines the vision, mission, target audience, marketing strategies and financial projections. This document serves as a road map that guides the growth of the main hustle and minimizes uncertainties.

Adopting an entrepreneurial mindset:

The shift to mainstream is not just a shift in income streams; it's a mindset shift towards business. Adopting an entrepreneurial mindset involves adaptability, resilience and a willingness to learn.

Continuous self-improvement, following industry trends, and networking play a key role in ensuring continued success.

Navigating challenges and learning curves:
The journey from the side hustle to the main hustle is rarely without problems. Adapting to a heavier workload, managing finances effectively and coping with uncertainty require resilience and problem-solving skills. Learning from failures and using them as opportunities for growth is critical to long-term success.

Evaluating potential income streams when transitioning from side hustle to main hustle is a multifaceted process that requires a combination of financial acumen, market awareness, and a resilient entrepreneurial mindset. By carefully assessing profitability, market demand, scalability, and personal fulfillment, individuals can make informed decisions that pave the way for a successful and sustainable main hustle. Balancing risks, building a solid foundation and adopting an entrepreneurial mindset are critical elements in navigating the complexities of this transformational journey. When individuals embark on this journey, they are not only redefining their approach to work, but also contributing to the evolving landscape of modern employment.

2.4 Balancing Passion and Profitability

In the dynamic environment of modern business, the concept of a side hustle has gained immense popularity. Many individuals are driven by the desire to turn their passion into a profitable business while still juggling the security of a full-time job. But as ambitions grow, the transition from side hustle to main hustle becomes a pivotal moment that requires careful consideration of the delicate balance between passion and profitability.

Passionate start:
The journey often begins with a passion project, a side hustle born out of genuine interest and enthusiasm. Whether it's a creative activity, a

skills-based service or a niche product, the initial focus revolves around enjoying what one loves. However, the shift to the main hustle requires a broader perspective, beyond the personal joy of meeting the demands of the market.

Understanding profitability:
Profitability is the cornerstone of any successful business, and transitioning to the mainstream requires a realistic assessment of financial viability. While passion is a driving force, it must be harmoniously combined with a good understanding of market trends, customer needs and revenue potential. Calculating costs, setting competitive prices and creating a sustainable business model become necessary steps.

Strategic transition planning:
Successfully transitioning from side hustle to main hustle requires strategic planning. Setting clear goals, timelines and milestones helps steer the business towards long-term sustainability. This phase requires a shift from the relatively flexible nature of the side hustle to a more structured and

organized approach that aligns with the demands of a full-fledged business.

Risk Mitigation:
Passion often drives risk-taking, but making the leap to the mainstream requires a thoughtful approach. Risk identification and mitigation become key components of the transition process. This includes creating contingency plans, building financial reserves, and diversifying income streams to weather the uncertainties that come with growing a business.

Building a strong brand identity:
On the way from side hustle to main hustle, the brand evolves from a personal project to a recognized entity. Developing a strong brand identity becomes paramount, including a professional image, effective marketing strategies and a commitment to delivering value. Consistency across all business aspects builds trust and credibility, which are essential elements for sustained profitability.

Balancing time and energy:

As the commitment to the business intensifies, balancing time and energy becomes a challenging task. Prioritizing tasks, delegating responsibilities, and maintaining a healthy work-life balance become critical to preventing burnout. The transition requires a rethinking of time management strategies to ensure that both passion and profitability aspects are given adequate attention.

Adapting to market changes:

Markets are dynamic and successful entrepreneurs adapt to change. The transition period requires careful monitoring of market trends, consumer behavior and emerging technologies. Flexibility and adaptability are key attributes as a business evolves from a side project to a full-time enterprise. Staying on top ensures continued relevance and competitiveness.

Cultivating a growth mindset:

Making the transition to the main hustle requires a mindset shift from hobbyist to business owner. Adopting a growth mindset involves a willingness to learn, adapt and innovate. Continuing education, seeking mentorship and networking within the industry contribute to personal and professional development and foster a mindset that leads to long-term success.

Overcoming challenges:
Challenges are inevitable on the entrepreneurial journey. Whether it's financial setbacks, market competition, or internal struggles, overcoming challenges requires resilience. Moving to the main hustle amplifies the impact of obstacles, so persistence and a positive mindset are key to managing the complexities of business.

Balancing passion and profitability while transitioning from side hustle to main hustle is a multifaceted endeavor. It requires a delicate dance between the intrinsic joy of pursuing one's passion and the pragmatic considerations of running a successful business. By planning strategically, mitigating risk, building a strong brand, managing time effectively, adapting to market changes, cultivating a growth mindset, and overcoming challenges, entrepreneurs can navigate this transition with confidence and turn their passion into a sustainable and profitable side hustle.

Chapter 3: Building and Growing Your Side Hustle

Building and growing a side hustle can be a transformative journey that often begins as a passion project or means of supplementing income. When individuals dive into the world of side hustles, they experience challenges, learn valuable skills, and in some cases, see their side hustle evolve into a major source of income. This transition from side hustle to main hustle involves strategic planning, determination, and a good understanding of market dynamics.

I. The Genesis of a Side Hustle

A. Identifying passions and opportunities:
The beginning of a side hustle often stems from personal passions or from identifying an unmet

need in the market. Whether it's freelancing, selling handmade crafts, or providing services, individuals find joy and meaning in activities outside of their primary occupation.

B. Balancing Act: Time and Commitment Management:
For many, juggling a side hustle alongside a full-time job requires effective time management. Finding the right balance ensures that the side hustle doesn't compromise the quality of work at the main job while also supporting the growth of the entrepreneurial endeavor.

II. Taking care of your side hustle

A. Learning and skills development:
When individuals delve deeper into their side hustle, they often acquire new skills and expand their knowledge base. This continuous learning process not only increases the quality of their offering, but also increases confidence and adaptability.

B. Branding and online presentation:

Creating a strong online presence is critical to growing a side hustle. Creating a professional website, leveraging social media platforms and using effective marketing strategies contribute to brand visibility and customer engagement.

C. Financial management:

Sound financial practices are vital to sustaining and growing a side hustle. Implementing budget strategies, tracking income and expenses, and reinvesting profits back into the business are key components of financial management.

III. Turning Point: Side to Main

A. Recognizing market trends:

Successful transitions from side hustle to main hustle often involve keen observation of market trends. Understanding the demand for products or services and adapting to change positions a business for long-term viability.

B. Scaling operation:

As the side hustle gains momentum, entrepreneurs may need to scale operations to meet increased demand. This may include hiring additional staff, investing in technology, or expanding product and service offerings.

C. Risk and reward assessment:
Moving to the main hustle comes with risks and rewards. Entrepreneurs must consider factors such as financial stability, market competition and personal readiness to make informed decisions about making the leap.

IV. Strategies for a successful transition

A. Strategic planning:
A well-thought-out transition plan is essential. This includes setting clear goals, identifying potential challenges and developing strategies to mitigate risks. A step-by-step approach can make the process easier and increase the chances of success.

B. Networking and collaboration:

Building a robust network within an industry can open doors for collaboration and partnership. Leveraging relationships with peers, mentors, and industry influencers can provide valuable insights and support during the transition.

C. Marketing and branding overhaul:
As the side hustle turns into the main hustle, a comprehensive rethinking of marketing and branding strategies is often necessary. This may include redefining the target audience, refreshing brand elements and adopting larger marketing campaigns.

V. Navigating challenges and celebrating success

A. Overcoming Challenges:
The journey from the side hustle to the main hustle is not without problems. Coping with challenges such as increased workloads, financial pressures and potential burnout requires resilience and adaptability.

B. Celebrating Milestones:

In the midst of challenges, it is crucial to recognize and celebrate milestones. Whether it's hitting a revenue goal, expanding your customer base, or launching a new product, recognizing accomplishments boosts morale and motivation.

Building and growing a side hustle into a main hustle is a testament to an individual's entrepreneurial spirit and determination. It includes a dynamic process of learning, adaptation and strategic positioning of the company in the market. By embracing challenges and celebrating successes, entrepreneurs can successfully navigate this transition and turn their passion projects into a sustainable side hustle.

3.1 Establishing a Solid Foundation

Building a solid foundation is essential when transitioning from side hustle to main hustle. This journey involves transforming a part-time passion project into a full-fledged, sustainable business. By laying a solid foundation, individuals can manage challenges, seize opportunities, and build a thriving business. This article explores key elements of this development and provides insight into strategic planning, financial management, branding and personal development.

Strategic planning:
Careful strategic planning is paramount before taking the leap. Define clear goals, evaluate market trends and identify your target audience. Understanding your niche and competition will allow you to create a unique space for your business. Create a comprehensive business plan that outlines your mission, vision and strategy. This document will become your road map to guide you in your decisions and actions as you move from side gig to main hustle.

Financial management:
A solid financial foundation is the backbone of any successful business. Assess your current financial problems and predict future income and expenses. Create a budget that covers business operations, marketing and personal needs. Consider setting aside an emergency fund to mitigate unexpected setbacks. Understanding the financial health of

your business will allow you to make informed decisions and ensure stability during the transition.

Branding and Marketing:
When you go from a side project to a full-time business, branding becomes a key driver of success. Create a compelling brand identity that resonates with your target audience. This includes a memorable logo, consistent messaging and a strong online presence. Use social media, content marketing and networking to strengthen your brand. Invest time in building relationships with clients and colleagues to increase your market reach.

Team Building:
Expanding from a solo operation to a team requires careful consideration. Assess tasks that can be delegated and hire individuals to complement your skills. A cohesive team boosts productivity and creativity, enabling businesses to thrive. Create clear communication channels and cultivate a positive work environment to foster collaboration and innovation.

Legal Aspects:

Make sure your business meets all legal requirements. This includes registering your business, obtaining the necessary licenses and understanding tax obligations. Protect your intellectual property by securing trademarks or patents where applicable. Compliance with the law from the very beginning protects your business from possible complications.

Full Time Commitment Adjustment:

Moving to the main hustle requires a change in mindset and lifestyle. Make the commitment needed to make the business a success. Create a structured work routine and set boundaries to maintain a healthy work-life balance. Stay adaptable, be ready to change strategies based on market feedback, and continually invest in your skills to stay relevant in your industry.

Feedback and Repeat Customers:

Collecting and integrating customer feedback is an ongoing process. Listen to your clients, analyze market trends and be ready to iterate on your products or services. This adaptability ensures that your business remains relevant and customer-centric, which promotes long-term success.

Risk management:
Be aware that doing business carries risks. Mitigate them by diversifying your income streams, conducting thorough market research, and being financially prudent. An established risk management strategy allows you to move flexibly in the face of uncertainty.

Scaling:
Once the foundations are solid, explore opportunities to expand your business. This may include expanding product lines, entering new markets, or implementing efficient systems to handle increased demand. A well-thought-out scaling strategy ensures sustained growth without compromising quality.

Personal development:

Investing in personal development is an integral part of a successful transition to the main hustle. Hone your skills, stay up-to-date on industry trends, and seek mentorship. Continuous learning not only increases your skills, but also positions you as a leader in your field.

Building a solid foundation when transitioning from your side hustle to your main hustle is a multi-faceted journey. Strategic planning, financial management, branding, team building, legal aspects, commitment, customer feedback, risk management and personal development together form the pillars of this foundation. By carefully addressing each aspect, budding entrepreneurs can overcome the challenges of this transition and set the stage for a thriving and sustainable business.

3.2 Effective Time Management Strategies

When transitioning from side hustle to main hustle, effective time management is essential. Balancing multiple responsibilities requires strategic planning and disciplined execution. In this comprehensive guide, we'll explore key time management strategies that can enable individuals to make this shift, help them optimize productivity, maintain work-life balance, and achieve success in both their side hustles and their main pursuits.

Understanding transition:

The journey from side hustle to main hustle often involves a significant increase in responsibility and time pressure. Recognizing this transition is the first step to effective time management. Realize that what was once a supplemental source of income is evolving into a primary focus and requires a more structured approach to the use of time.

Establishing priorities and goals:

Set clear priorities by identifying the tasks that contribute most to your overall goals. Set short-term and long-term goals to guide your efforts. This not only provides a plan for your activities, but also helps you stay motivated and focused on what really matters.

Time blocking techniques:

Implementing time blocking can be a game changer. Allocate specific blocks of time to different tasks or categories of work. This helps prevent multitasking and allows you to give your full attention to one aspect of your hustle at a time. For example, designate the morning for your side hustle and the afternoon for your main hustle.

Efficient task management tools:

Use technology to streamline your workflow. Use task management tools like Trello, Asana, or Notion to organize to-do lists, set deadlines, and collaborate with others when needed. These tools can increase efficiency, reduce stress, and provide a visual representation of your progress.

Introduction of the routine:

Creating a consistent daily or weekly routine promotes discipline and helps you manage your time effectively. A well-structured routine minimizes decision fatigue and ensures you're allocating time where it's most needed without constantly reassessing. Be flexible, but maintain a basic routine that aligns with your goals.

Learning to say "no":
As your commitments grow, it becomes essential to learn to say "no" when necessary. Overcommitment can lead to burnout and negatively affect the quality of your work. Prioritize tasks and be realistic about what you can take without compromising your well-being.

Delegation and outsourcing:
Be aware of your strengths and weaknesses. Delegating tasks that are outside of your expertise or that can be handled by others allows you to focus on high-priority activities. Outsourcing certain aspects of your work, such as administrative tasks or specific projects, can also be a strategic and time-saving move.

Effective communication:
Open and transparent communication is vital, especially if you work with others or manage a team. Be clear about your expectations, deadlines

and any challenges you may face. This ensures that everyone is on the same page and can contribute to a collaborative and supportive work environment.

Continuous learning and skill development:
Investing time in continuous learning can improve your skills and effectiveness. Stay informed about industry trends, tools and techniques relevant to your hustle. This proactive approach not only makes you more competent, but also allows you to find innovative solutions that can save time in the long run.

Mindfulness and self-care:
Balancing your side hustle and your main hustle requires sustained energy and focus. Incorporate mindfulness practices and self-care routines into your schedule. Whether it's meditation, exercise, or hobbies, taking time for yourself contributes to overall well-being and can improve your productivity when you return to work.

Regular evaluation and modification:

Regularly evaluate your time management strategies. Think about what is working well and what could be improved. Be open to adjusting your approach as your side hustle evolves into your main hustle. Flexibility and adaptability are key components of effective time management.

Moving from side hustle to main hustle requires a conscious effort to manage your time effectively. By implementing prioritization techniques, adopting effective tools, establishing routines, and encouraging effective communication, individuals can navigate this shift successfully. Remember that the journey is dynamic and requires constant learning and adaptation. With a comprehensive approach to time management, you can not only thrive in your side hustles and main hustles, but also maintain a fulfilling work-life balance.

3.3 Marketing and Branding for Side Hustles

In the dynamic world of business, side hustles have become a cornerstone for many individuals seeking financial independence and pursuing their passion projects. As these side gigs develop and gain momentum, the transition from supplemental income to full-fledged mainstay becomes a natural progression. However, this journey requires strategic marketing and branding efforts to successfully navigate the competitive business landscape. In this survey, we dive into the key aspects of side hustle marketing and branding and reveal a blueprint for entrepreneurs who want to turn their side gigs into thriving main businesses.

Understanding the Side Hustle landscape:

A side hustle often starts as a passion or means of supplementing income. Entrepreneurs can start by offering products or services on a small scale, testing the waters to gauge market interest. At this initial stage, the emphasis is usually on providing value to a specific audience. Marketing efforts are simple, relying on word of mouth, social media presence and basic online platforms.

As a side hustle gains traction, transitioning to a mainstream business requires a mindset shift. Entrepreneurs must evolve from viewing their business as a hobby to treating it as a serious business. This shift lays the foundation for comprehensive marketing and branding strategies that will take the side hustle to the next level.

Building a strong brand identity:
Effective branding is the foundation of any successful business. As the side hustle matures, entrepreneurs need to define and refine their brand identity to resonate with a wider audience. This includes creating a compelling brand story, creating a unique value proposition and creating a memorable visual identity.

One of the key elements in this process is the development of a distinctive brand personality. Whether it's through tone of voice in communications, visual aesthetics or a unique selling proposition, a strong brand personality differentiates the competition from the competition. This differentiation is essential as the business expands and faces increased market saturation.

Strategic Marketing for Growth:
Marketing for side hustles on their way to becoming a main hustle requires a strategic approach. The

focus is shifting from individual transactions to building customer relationships and long-term engagement. Businesses need to use different channels, both online and offline, to reach and connect with their target audience.

Digital marketing is increasingly important at this stage. Social media platforms, content marketing, and email campaigns can exponentially increase the reach of a side hustle. Engaging content that tells a brand story and demonstrates the value of products or services is key. In addition, search engine optimization (SEO) and online advertising can significantly increase visibility in a crowded digital market.

Data-driven decision making:

With growing side traffic, data becomes a valuable asset in refining marketing strategies. Businesses should use analytics tools to gather information about customer behavior, monitor marketing performance, and identify areas for improvement. Data-driven decision-making enables better understanding of target audiences and ensures that marketing efforts are optimized for maximum impact.

Diversification of marketing channels:
While digital channels are powerful, a holistic marketing strategy for a side hustle transitioning into a main hustle should include a combination of online and offline channels. Networking events, partnerships and collaborations can improve brand visibility within the local community. This diversified approach helps mitigate the risks associated with relying on just one marketing channel and enables a more comprehensive reach.

Investment in professionalism:
As the side hustle turns into the main hustle, the level of professionalism in both branding and marketing becomes paramount. Businesses should invest in professional branding materials, including a polished logo, consistent visuals, and high-quality marketing materials. Professionalism not only increases credibility, but also positions the brand for partnerships and collaborations with other businesses.

Customer-oriented approach:

The customer should always be at the forefront of marketing and branding efforts. With side hustles on the rise, maintaining a customer-centric approach is even more important. Soliciting and responding to customer feedback, providing excellent customer service, and tailoring marketing strategies based on customer preferences contribute to long-term success.

On the journey from side hustle to main hustle, the importance of effective marketing and branding cannot be overstated. As entrepreneurs go through this transition, a strategic and adaptive approach to these aspects is essential. Building a strong brand identity, making data-driven decisions, diversifying marketing channels, and maintaining a customer-centric focus are key elements that contribute to sustained side hustle growth.

By combining creativity, strategy, and a commitment to professionalism, entrepreneurs can turn their side gigs into a thriving main hustle and cement their place in the competitive business landscape. As this journey evolves, constant learning and adapting to market trends will be essential to ensure the brand remains relevant and resilient in the face of evolving challenges.

3.4 Leveraging Online Platforms and Networking

Leveraging online platforms and networking is key to transitioning from side hustle to main. In a digital age where connectivity is ubiquitous, individuals can harness the power of various online tools and networks to fuel their entrepreneurial journey. This comprehensive survey delves into the strategic use of online platforms and networks to maximize opportunities, drive growth, and ultimately turn a side hustle into a thriving main hustle.

The foundation of this transformation lies in choosing the right online platforms tailored to the nature of the side hustle. Whether it's ecommerce platforms like Shopify, freelance websites like Upwork, or social media channels like Instagram, each platform offers distinct advantages. Creating a thoughtful online presence and leveraging the features of these platforms can greatly expand your reach and attract a wider audience.

Building a robust personal brand is just as important. Networking on professional platforms like LinkedIn allows for meaningful connections with colleagues, mentors, and potential clients. Active participation in relevant groups and forums creates opportunities for collaboration and knowledge sharing and fosters a supportive community around the side hustle.

Using social media effectively is a game changer. Platforms like Twitter, Facebook and LinkedIn can be used not only for promotion but also for building authentic relationships. Engaging content, consistent posting schedules, and genuine interaction with followers can contribute to a growing and loyal audience and increase the visibility of your side hustle.

Strategic collaboration is another avenue to explore. Partnering with other entrepreneurs or influencers in the same field can expose a side hustle to a wider audience. Joint ventures, co-hosted events, or co-creation of content can yield win-win results and accelerate the transition from side gig to main hustle.

A key element of this journey is investment in online education and skills development. Various e-learning platforms provide opportunities to acquire new skills or enhance existing ones, enabling individuals to offer greater value within their field. Continuous learning not only increases expertise, but also increases credibility and marketability.

The use of data analysis tools is essential for informed decision making. Understanding customer behavior, market trends and KPIs enables strategic adjustments and improvements. This data-driven approach is helpful in growing your side hustle and making it sustainable as it turns into your main hustle.

Automation is a critical component in managing the increased workload that comes with the transition to the mainstream. Implementing tools for tasks like email marketing, customer relationship management, and social media planning frees up time for strategic planning and business development.

As the side hustle gains momentum, financial management becomes critical. Adopting online accounting tools helps in tracking income, expenses and overall financial health. Clear financial overviews enable better decision-making and ensure the long-term viability of the business.

The journey from side hustle to main hustle is a dynamic process that requires a multifaceted approach. Strategic use of online platforms and networking enables entrepreneurs to expand their reach, build a strong community, and position their businesses for sustained success in the digital environment. With a combination of an effective online presence, skill development, collaboration, data-driven decision-making, and effective management, individuals can navigate this transition with confidence and turn their side hustle into a thriving main hustle.

Chapter 4 Navigating Challenges and Risks

Going from a side hustle to becoming your main source of income is an exciting yet challenging task. As more and more individuals explore the realm of entrepreneurship, the journey from part-time passion to full-time commitment requires careful navigation through a myriad of challenges and risks. In this comprehensive guide, we delve into the complexities of this transition and provide insights, strategies and real-world examples to help budding entrepreneurs on their journey.

Understanding the landscape:
The first step in navigating this transition is gaining a deep understanding of the business environment. Analyzing market trends, identifying your target audience, and evaluating the scalability of your side hustle are key considerations. Thorough market

analysis allows you to make informed decisions, mitigating the risks associated with entering a competitive arena or targeting an oversaturated market.

Financial readiness:

The financial aspect is a critical consideration when transitioning from a side hustle to a main one. Creating a robust financial base requires careful budgeting, creating an emergency fund and understanding cash flow dynamics. Diversifying income streams and exploring potential funding options such as loans or investors can provide additional support during the early stages of the transition.

Time management and burnout:

With increasing demands on your time, effective time management becomes paramount. Balancing a full-time job with a side hustle takes discipline and prioritization. Recognizing the signs of burnout and implementing strategies to prevent it are key to maintaining long-term success. This can include setting boundaries, delegating tasks, and adopting a healthy work-life balance.

Building a strong brand:
A successful transition is largely dependent on building a strong and recognizable brand. Creating a compelling brand identity, including a memorable logo, consistent messaging and a robust online presence, increases visibility and credibility. Utilizing social media platforms, content marketing and networking are all integral parts of branding and contributing to a positive perception of your business.

Legal and regulatory aspects:
Navigating the legal and regulatory landscape is often overlooked, but can be a key aspect of transitioning to the mainstream. Registering your business, obtaining the necessary licenses and understanding your tax obligations are essential steps. Consulting with legal professionals can help ensure compliance and protect your business from potential legal pitfalls.

Customer acquisition and retention:

A successful transition requires a solid customer acquisition and retention strategy. Understanding your target audience, identifying effective marketing channels and implementing customer-centric practices contribute to sustainable growth. Building strong relationships with customers not only fosters loyalty, but also creates positive word of mouth, a powerful tool for organic business growth.

Scaling operations:

Scaling a side hustle into a main hustle requires strategic planning and operational efficiency. Scalability assessment includes assessment of production capacity, supply chain logistics and workforce capabilities. Implementing scalable technologies and processes enables your business to grow while minimizing operational risk.

Adapting to market dynamics:

The business environment is dynamic and adapting to market changes is a constant challenge. Keeping track of industry trends, keeping up with technological advancements and reacting agilely to market changes is essential. Businesses that can pivot and innovate in response to changing circumstances are better positioned to meet challenges and seize new opportunities.

Case studies and success stories:
Drawing inspiration from real case studies and success stories can provide valuable insights. Analyzing how other entrepreneurs have dealt with challenges, overcome setbacks and achieved success can offer guidance and inspiration. Learning from both triumphs and failures will strengthen your decision making and prepare you to face unforeseen challenges.

Going from side hustle to main hustle is a transformational process that requires resilience, strategic thinking, and a commitment to continuous improvement. By understanding the environment, managing finances effectively, building a strong brand and adapting to market dynamics, aspiring entrepreneurs can navigate challenges and risks with confidence. This comprehensive guide serves as a road map for individuals to turn their side hustle dreams into a thriving main hustle reality.

4.1 Financial Management in Side Hustles

Financial management in the context of transitioning from side hustle to main hustle is a critical aspect of ensuring long-term success and sustainability. Many individuals start side businesses as a means of supplementing their income or exploring their business interests. However, as these side businesses grow and develop, effective financial management becomes increasingly important. This article dives into the various aspects of financial management on the side, exploring key principles, challenges and strategies for making a smooth transition from side hustle to main hustle.

Understanding Financial Management in Side Hustles

1. Budget and Planning:

Financial success starts with a solid budget. Side issues often start small, but as they grow, so do the financial complexities. Creating a detailed budget that takes into account both fixed and variable expenses helps individuals gain a clear picture of their financial health. It also helps in setting realistic financial goals for the transition to the main hustle.

2. Income Diversification:

Relying solely on a single income stream from a side hustle can present risks. Diversification of income sources not only reduces risks, but also provides a more stable financial base. This may include expanding product or service offerings, targeting new customer segments, or exploring additional revenue streams within an existing business model.

3. Profitability Analysis:

Assessing the profitability of a side hustle is critical. In addition to gross revenue, it is important to understand net profit margins and identify areas for cost optimization. Regular analysis of financial statements helps entrepreneurs make informed decisions and ensures that the business is financially sustainable.

4. Emergency fund and risk management:

Unforeseen challenges are inevitable in business. Building an emergency fund to cover unexpected expenses provides a safety net during times of financial uncertainty. In addition, having insurance or risk mitigation strategies protects business and personal finances.

Challenges in financial management during the transformation

1. Scaling Expenses:

As side traffic grows, so do expenses. Managing this scaling process is critical. Business owners must carefully evaluate which expenses directly contribute to growth and sustainability and which may require adjustment to maintain financial health.

2. Tax Compliance:

The tax implications become more complex when the side hustle turns into a major source of income. Understanding your tax obligations, complying with regulations and taking advantage of available tax benefits are essential to maintaining financial stability and avoiding legal problems.

3. Cash Flow Management:

Maintaining a healthy cash flow is challenging during transitions. Delayed payments or unexpected expenses can put a strain on finances. Implementing effective invoicing, tracking payments and negotiating favorable terms with suppliers are strategies to ensure positive cash flow.

4. Balancing personal and business finances:

Going from a side hustle to a main hustle often involves a change in mindset. Entrepreneurs must find a balance between personal and business finances. Setting clear boundaries and separating personal and business expenses is essential for financial clarity.

Strategies for a smooth transition

1. Professional financial advice:

Seeking advice from financial professionals can provide valuable insights. Accountants, financial advisors or business consultants can offer advice tailored to the specific needs of a growing hustle.

2. Investments in systems and technologies:

The implementation of robust financial systems and the use of technology can make financial management processes more efficient. Automated accounting tools, invoicing platforms and financial analysis software can increase efficiency and accuracy.

3. Continuous Learning:

The financial environment is dynamic and regulation is evolving. Entrepreneurs should invest time in continuous learning to stay abreast of financial trends, tax laws and best practices. This knowledge enables them to make informed decisions.

4. Incremental Scaling:

Rather than rushing into a full-time business, consider scaling up gradually. This allows for a smoother transition and gives the entrepreneur time to adjust to the increased demands on their time and resources.

On the journey from side hustle to main hustle, effective financial management is the cornerstone of success. It involves careful planning, adaptability and a proactive approach to challenges. Entrepreneurs must become financially literate, seek professional advice when needed and constantly improve their financial strategies. By comprehensively addressing the financial aspects, individuals can navigate the transition with confidence and ensure the long-term viability and prosperity of their main hustle.

4.2 Balancing Side Hustles with Main Job Responsibilities

Balancing side hustles with primary work responsibilities is a delicate juggling act that many individuals undertake in an effort to diversify their income streams and pursue their passions. Going from side hustle to main hustle is a major milestone that requires careful planning, time management, and a strategic approach. In this survey, we'll delve into the challenges and benefits of managing side hustles alongside your primary job responsibilities, and explore the key factors that contribute to a successful transition from side hustle to full-fledged career.

Landscape Understanding:
The modern work environment is evolving and more and more individuals are looking for alternative ways to express their skills, creativity and entrepreneurial spirit. Side hustles, often initiated as a passion or additional sources of income, can grow into significant endeavors that challenge the traditional definition of a "main job." The journey from side hustle to main hustle involves navigating a maze of time constraints, financial considerations, and personal commitments.

Challenges we face while balancing side hustles:
One of the main challenges when managing side hustles with your main job is time management. Balancing the demands of a full-time job and devoting enough energy to a side hustle requires

careful planning and discipline. In addition, individuals may experience burnout when trying to meet the expectations of both career fields.

Financial stability is another aspect that individuals must carefully consider. Relying on your main job for a stable income can make it hard to fully commit to a side hustle at first. Additionally, the financial risks involved in moving from a secure job to a potentially unpredictable business venture can be daunting.

Juggling Benefits and Main Job Responsibilities:

Despite the challenges, managing a side hustle alongside your main job offers countless benefits. First, it provides a safety net during the initial stages of the business. Individuals can test the waters of their side hustle without completely leaving the security of their primary source of income.

Additionally, skills acquired in a side hustle often complement skills acquired in a main job. Cross-pollination of experiences can lead to a more well-rounded skill set, enhancing the overall professional profile. Additionally, successful side hustles can eventually evolve into a main hustle that offers individuals the freedom to pursue their passions full-time.

Leveling and Transition Strategies:
A strategic approach is necessary to successfully navigate the journey from side hustle to main hustle. Setting clear goals and timelines for growing your side hustle is essential. This includes identifying key milestones and gradually allocating more time and resources to the business effort as it progresses.

Effective time management is a fundamental pillar of balancing multiple responsibilities. Creating a well-structured schedule that allocates specific blocks of time to main work and side hustles helps maintain clarity and prevents burnout. Utilizing productivity tools and techniques can increase efficiency and streamline workflows.

Financial planning is equally important. Building a financial cushion before jumping into a full-time business provides a safety net. It is advisable to reinvest the profits from the side hustle into its growth while maintaining financial stability through the main job.

Case studies and success stories:
Examining real-life examples of individuals who have successfully transitioned from side hustle to main hustle can offer valuable insights. Highlighting cases where careful planning, resilience and strategic decision-making led to flourishing entrepreneurial activities can inspire others considering a similar path.

Balancing side hustles with your main work responsibilities is a complex endeavor that requires dedication, strategic planning, and resilience. Transitioning from a supplemental source of income to a full-fledged career requires a thoughtful approach that takes into account time management, financial stability, and personal well-being. By embracing the challenges and reaping the benefits, individuals can successfully navigate this path and turn their side hustle into a fulfilling main hustle that aligns with their passions and professional ambitions.

4.3 Dealing with Competition and Market Changes

Orientation in the competition and changes in the market is a crucial aspect of the transition from the side hustle to the main hustle. When entrepreneurs make this leap, they encounter a dynamic environment that requires adaptability, strategic planning, and a good understanding of market forces. In this survey, we delve into the complexities of coping with competition and market changes while expanding on the side hustle.

Acceptance of competition

1. Market analysis and research:

Do a thorough analysis of your industry. Understand your competitors, their strengths and weaknesses, and their market position. This knowledge forms the basis for creating strategies that will differentiate your main hustle.

2. Strategy of differentiation:

Find out what makes your business different. Whether it's unique products, exceptional customer service or innovative solutions, a differentiated value proposition helps you stand out in the competitive environment.

3. Constant Innovation:

Embrace a culture of continuous improvement and innovation. Stay ahead by regularly updating your products or services to meet changing consumer preferences and emerging market trends.

4. Agile Marketing:

Create an agile marketing strategy that allows you to quickly respond to changes in the market. This means being flexible with your campaigns and promotions to stay relevant and take advantage of new opportunities.

Adapting to market changes

1. Monitoring market trends:

Keep a close eye on market trends. Subscribe to industry publications, attend relevant events, and use market research tools to stay informed about changes in consumer behavior, technology, and economic factors.

2. Customer feedback and engagement:

Foster strong relationships with your customers. Collect feedback regularly to understand their evolving needs and expectations. This not only builds customer loyalty, but also provides valuable insights to tailor your offers.

3. Flexibility in operations:

Build flexibility into your business operations. This may include agile supply chain management, scalable manufacturing processes or versatile service offerings. Agility allows you to quickly adapt to market fluctuations.

4. Financial prudence:

Maintain a strong financial strategy. Having reserves and a clear understanding of your financial health will ensure you can handle economic downturns or unexpected market challenges.

Transition from secondary to main activity

1. Strategic planning:

Outline a clear transition plan. This includes setting specific goals, timelines and key performance indicators (KPIs) to measure progress. A well-defined plan provides a structured approach to expansion.

2. Resource Allocation:

Assess your resource needs for scaling. This includes financial resources, personnel, technology and infrastructure. Effectively allocate resources to support the increased demands of the main hustle.

3. Risk Management:

Recognize and mitigate potential risks. This can range from changes in market regulations to unexpected competitive moves. A robust risk management strategy protects your business during the transition.

4. Team Building and Leadership:

As your side hustle develops, invest in building a strong team. Effective leadership becomes crucial at this stage. Cultivate a positive and collaborative work culture that moves your core business forward.

Going from side hustle to main hustle is a transformational process that requires resilience, foresight, and strategic thinking. Dealing with competition and market changes becomes a constant challenge, but with the right mindset and proactive approach, entrepreneurs can not only survive but thrive in the ever-evolving business environment. Embrace competition as a driver for improvement, stay agile in adapting to market changes, and carefully plan your transition to ensure continued success on your major challenge journey.

4.4 Legal and Regulatory Considerations

Turning a side hustle into a main hustle is an exciting venture that requires careful consideration of legal and regulatory aspects. As entrepreneurs embark on this journey, it is critical to navigate the complex landscape to ensure compliance, protect assets and drive sustainable growth. This contextual content explores the key legal and regulatory aspects associated with moving from the side hustle to the mainstream.

1. Business Structure:
Choosing the right business structure is a fundamental step. Sole proprietorship, partnership, LLC, or corporation - each has different legal implications. Sole proprietorships and partnerships offer simplicity, but expose personal assets to business liabilities. LLCs and corporations provide liability protection but require more formalities. Assessing the nature of the business and consulting with legal professionals can guide entrepreneurs in making informed decisions.

2. Registration and License:

The transition to the main hustle often requires the formalization of the business through registration with the relevant authorities. This includes obtaining the necessary licenses and permits, which vary by location and industry. Compliance with local, state, and federal regulations is essential to avoid legal consequences and foster a trustworthy business reputation.

3. Compliance with tax obligations:

As the scale of operations increases, tax obligations become more complex. Entrepreneurs must be aware of their income tax, sales tax and employment tax obligations. Tax compliance not only ensures legal compliance, but also prevents financial setbacks. Working with tax professionals can provide valuable insights and help optimize tax strategies.

4. Labor laws:

Business expansion may involve hiring employees. Compliance with employment laws, including fair labor standards, non-discrimination and workplace safety, is essential. Concluding clear employment contracts, ensuring a safe working environment and complying with wage laws contribute to a legally sound and ethical business.

5. Intellectual property protection:
Protecting intellectual property becomes more critical in the transition to the mainstream. Trademarks, copyrights, and patents protect unique assets, products, or services. Conducting thorough reviews and filings, as well as monitoring for potential violations, are critical steps to avoid litigation and protect brand integrity.

6. Contracts and Agreements:
Clear and well-drafted contracts are the foundation of a successful main hustle. Whether you are dealing with clients, suppliers or partners, formal agreements reduce the risk of misunderstandings and legal disputes. Businesses should seek legal

advice when drafting contracts to ensure enforceability and protection of their interests.

7. Data protection and privacy:

As your business grows, handling customer and employee data becomes a significant responsibility. Compliance with data protection laws and ensuring the privacy of sensitive information is paramount. Implementing robust cybersecurity measures, privacy policies and obtaining consent to data processing are essential components of legal compliance.

8. Regulatory Compliance:

Industries may be subject to specific regulations and standards. Entrepreneurs must stay abreast of changes in their respective industries and adapt their operations accordingly. Compliance not only prevents legal problems, but also demonstrates a commitment to ethical business practices.

9. Financial reporting:

With growth comes increased scrutiny of financial practices. Accurate and transparent financial reporting is essential to comply with legal regulations and gain investor confidence. Adhering to accounting standards and seeking expert advice on financial matters contributes to the overall health and legality of the business.

10. Insurance coverage:

Extending the side hustle to the main hustle increases the importance of insurance coverage. Whether it's general liability, professional indemnity or property insurance, adequate coverage mitigates risk and protects the business against unforeseen events.

Going from side hustle to main hustle is a significant leap that requires careful consideration of legal and regulatory considerations. Entrepreneurs should proactively address these aspects to build a solid foundation for their growing businesses. Seeking professional legal advice during this process is a prudent strategy to deal with complex situations and ensure a legally resilient and prosperous business.

Chapter 5: Transitioning from Side Hustle to Main Hustle

Moving from side hustle to main hustle is a significant step on the entrepreneurial journey that marks a shift from a side hustle to a primary focus. This development requires careful planning, strategic decision-making and a deep understanding of market dynamics. In this survey, we dive into the key aspects of this transition and offer insights, tips, and considerations for successfully migrating from side gig to full-time job.

Understanding the Side Hustle landscape

1. Viability Assessment

- Assess the sustainability of your side hustle before you take the leap. Analyze market trends, customer demand and competition to ensure your business has a solid foundation.

2. Financial stability

- Evaluate your personal finances. Make sure you have a safety net to cover living expenses during the initial stages of transition when your main hustle may not immediately replace your current income.

Strategic Transition Planning

3. Organization of time

- Realize the time commitment required to run a full-time business. Create a realistic schedule that allows you to manage your side hustle and day-to-day work while gradually shifting your focus.

4. Refinement of the business plan*

- Reevaluate your business plan. Identify areas that need expansion or improvement and align your goals with the demands of a full-time business.

5. Building a Support System

- Surround yourself with mentors, advisors and a support network. Seek guidance from those who have successfully transitioned and use their experience to overcome challenges.

Financial Readiness

6. Revenue projection

- Create a realistic revenue projection for your main hustle. Consider different revenue streams, pricing strategies and potential challenges to create a robust financial plan.

7. Contingency Fund

- Create an emergency fund to mitigate unforeseen financial setbacks. This buffer provides a safety net during the initial stages when your main hustle may not generate consistent income.

Navigation in Challenges

8. Risk management

- Identify potential risks and develop mitigation strategies. This includes market fluctuations, changing consumer behavior and unexpected operational issues.

9. Adaptation to full-time responsibility

- Recognize the shift in responsibility. As a full-time entrepreneur, you will wear many different hats from marketing and sales to operations and customer service.

Marketing and Branding Strategies

10. Increase your brand

- Invest in branding efforts to differentiate your business in a competitive market. This can include enhancing your brand identity, improving your online presence and boosting customer engagement.

11. Marketing campaigns

- Develop comprehensive marketing campaigns that promote your core business. Use both online and offline channels to reach a wider audience and create a strong market presence.

Legal and Administrative Aspects

12. Business Structure

- Evaluate your business structure. Consider whether a change in legal structure is necessary for your main hustle. Consult legal counsel to ensure compliance.

13. tax consequences

- Understand the tax implications of switching to a full-time business. Consult a tax advisor to optimize your financial strategy and maximize deductions.

Monitoring progress and adaptation

14. Key Performance Indicators (KPIs)

- Define KPIs to measure the success of your main hustle. Monitor these indicators regularly to evaluate performance and adjust your strategies accordingly.

15. Continuous learning

- Stay informed about industry trends and business practices. Continuous learning is essential to adapt to market changes and maintain a competitive advantage.

16. Milestone Recognition

- Celebrate successes along the way. Recognize milestones, big and small, to boost morale and keep a positive mindset during the transition.

17. Change of mind

- Embrace the mindset shift from side hustler to full-time entrepreneur. This transition requires confidence, resilience and a willingness to learn from both successes and failures.

Going from side hustle to main hustle is a transformational journey that requires careful planning, resilience, and a commitment to continuous improvement. By understanding the complexities of this shift and implementing a well-thought-out strategy, budding entrepreneurs can manage the challenges, capitalize on the opportunities, and build a sustainable and thriving mainstream business.

5.1 Signs It's Time to Make the Transition

Making the transition from side hustle to main hustle is a major step that requires careful consideration and strategic planning. When you're navigating the business environment, there are a few signs that may indicate it's time to make that transition. Recognizing these signals can help you make informed decisions and maximize your chances of success.

1. Consistent Income Growth:

One clear indicator that it's time to turn your side hustle into your main hustle is consistent and substantial income growth. If your side gig is consistently outpacing your primary source of income, it could be a sign that your passion project has the potential to sustain you financially.

2. Passion overtakes primary work:

When your passion for your side hustle becomes more pronounced than your enthusiasm for your main job, it's a powerful sign that you're ready for a change. Feeling truly excited and fulfilled by your side project can be a driving force for success.

3. Limited time for both:

Balancing a side hustle and a full-time job can be challenging. If you find yourself struggling to split your time and energy between the two, it could be a sign that your side gig requires more commitment and deserves to be your main focus.

4. Market Validation and Demand:

Successful side hustles often attract attention and build a customer base. If you see increasing demand for your products or services and positive feedback from customers, this is a strong signal that there is a market for what you offer.

5. Stable clientele or customer base:

A stable and loyal clientele or customer base is the decisive factor. If you find that you have a consistent group of people who rely on your hustle, it suggests a level of stability that can support a full-time endeavor.

6. Bigger Opportunities:

As your side hustle grows, you may start receiving more opportunities such as partnerships, collaborations, or requests for extended services. This could indicate that your business is ready for more attention and commitment.

7. Personal and financial readiness:

Evaluate your personal and financial situation. If you've built up savings, have a clear understanding of your financial needs, and are mentally prepared for the challenges of running a full-time business, it may be the right time to take the leap.

8. Clear business plan and goals:

It is essential to have a well-defined business plan and achievable goals before making the transition. If you've outlined your strategy, identified your target markets, and set measurable goals, you're better positioned for success.

9. Feeling suffocated in current work:

If your current job is preventing you from following your passion and you feel restricted in your growth, it may be a sign that it's time to prioritize your side hustle. Feeling suffocated can be a motivating factor for change.

10. Network and Industry Recognition:

Recognition in your field and a growing professional network are positive signs. If your side hustle has gained credibility and respect, it's a sign that you've built something valuable and worth investing more time into.

Going from side hustle to main hustle is a big decision that requires careful consideration of various factors. Assessing your financial stability, passion, market demand and personal readiness are essential steps. By recognizing these signs and strategically planning your move, you can turn your passion project into a thriving full-time business. Remember that success often requires calculated risk and acceptance of change.

5.2 Financial Planning for the Transition

Financial planning during the transition from side hustle to main hustle is key to ensuring a smooth and successful transition in your professional endeavors. This transition period often involves a significant change in income, expenses, and overall financial stability. By strategically managing your finances, you can mitigate potential problems and position yourself for long-term success.

Understanding Transition:
The journey from side hustle to main hustle is both exciting and challenging. It means a shift from an additional source of income to a primary means of financial support. During this transition, it is essential to evaluate the financial implications and prepare for the changes that will come with relying on your main hustle for a living.

Assessment of current financial status:
Start by assessing your current financial situation. Take inventory of your side income, savings and

outstanding debt. This assessment will help you understand your starting point and identify areas that may require immediate attention. Consider creating a detailed budget that outlines your monthly income, fixed expenses, variable expenses, and savings goals.

Creating an emergency fund:
When you transition from your side hustle to your main hustle, a robust emergency fund plays an even more important role. Try to save at least three to six months of living expenses. This financial reserve can act as a safety net in the event of unexpected events, giving you the peace of mind you need to focus on growing your main hustle without financial stress.

Check and Adjust Expenses:
Switching to a main hustle can lead to changes in your income stream. Evaluate your current spending and identify areas where you can make adjustments. Cut back on non-essential expenses and focus on maintaining a modest lifestyle, at least

initially, to ensure financial stability during the transition.

Income Diversification:
Consider diversifying your income within your main hustle. Explore other income generating opportunities that align with your skills and interests. This can help create a more stable and resilient financial base and reduce dependence on a single source of income.

Debt Management:
Assess your existing debt and develop a strategy for managing it during the transition. Prioritize high-interest debts and work to pay them off to reduce your financial burden. A clear debt repayment plan will ensure that your main hustle income is maximized for wealth building rather than debt servicing.

Investment for the future:
When your main hustle becomes your primary source of income, shift your focus to long-term financial goals. Explore investment opportunities

that align with your risk tolerance and financial goals. Whether contributing to retirement accounts, investing in stocks or real estate, strategic investments can provide financial growth and security.

Insurance coverage:
Check your insurance coverage to make sure it is consistent with your new occupational status. Consider health, life and disability insurance options to protect yourself and your loved ones. Adequate coverage provides a safety net in the event of unforeseen circumstances, allowing you to handle challenges without jeopardizing your financial well-being.

Professional financial advice:
Consider seeking the advice of a financial adviser or financial adviser. A professional can provide personalized advice based on your unique circumstances and goals. They can help create a comprehensive financial plan, address tax implications and optimize your financial strategy during the transition.

Monitoring and Settings:

Monitor your financial progress regularly and be prepared to make adjustments as needed. Track your income, expenses and savings goals to stay on track. Being proactive in your financial management allows you to adapt to changing circumstances and make informed decisions.

Making the transition from side hustle to main hustle is a major step that requires careful financial planning. By evaluating your current financial situation, creating an emergency fund, reviewing and adjusting expenses, diversifying income, managing debt, investing wisely, securing insurance coverage, seeking professional advice and consistently monitoring your financial situation, you can navigate this transition successfully. Remember that strategic financial planning lays the foundation for a secure and prosperous future when you embrace your main hustle with confidence.

5.3 Communicating with Employers or Clients

Effective communication with employers or clients is key when transitioning from side hustle to main hustle. This shift requires not only a higher level of commitment and professionalism, but also requires clear and concise communication to foster positive relationships and ensure the success of your business.

As individuals embark on the journey of turning their side hustle into a major source of income, effective communication becomes a cornerstone of success. This transition is not just a shift in the amount of time invested; it is a transformation in thinking, determination and in the way of interaction with employers or clients.

Understanding Your Audience:
Before diving into effective communication strategies, it is essential to understand your audience. Employers and clients may have different communication expectations and preferences.

Tailoring your approach based on who you're dealing with can make a big difference in how your messages are received.

For employers, professionalism is often paramount. Clear and concise updates on your party's progress, along with a focus on the value you bring to the table, can strengthen your position. On the client's side, understanding their goals and expectations is essential. Regular reviews and transparent communication can build trust and foster collaboration.

Setting Clear Expectations:

Moving from side hustle to main hustle often involves a change in availability and deployment. Clearly communicating these changes is paramount to managing expectations. If your side hustle was initially something you did in your spare time, let your employer or clients know about your new availability and the increased commitment you are prepared to offer.

This communication should be proactive. Address potential concerns and offer solutions before they become problems. This demonstrates foresight and commitment to maintaining a positive working relationship.

Regular updates and progress reports:
In the world of side hustles, updates could be occasional, especially if it was a part-time job. When moving to the main hustle, regular updates become essential. These updates not only inform your employer or clients, but also showcase your dedication and progress.

Note the format of these updates. While some employers may prefer formal messages, others may appreciate a more informal but informative email. Tailoring your communication style to the recipient can increase the effectiveness of your updates.

Effective use of technology:
Use technology to make communication more efficient. Platforms such as project management tools, video conferencing and collaboration platforms can increase communication efficiency. This becomes especially important when handling

the more demanding workload associated with the main hustle.

Make sure you respond to messages and emails. Timely responses demonstrate reliability and a commitment to open communication. Use technology not only to communicate project updates, but also to actively engage your employer or clients about progress and any challenges you are facing.

Managing Feedback and Constructive Criticism:
As you move into the mainstream, the stakes are higher and constructive feedback becomes more important. Be open to feedback and see it as an opportunity for growth. Respond professionally and show a willingness to implement suggestions.

In cases where feedback is critical, approach the interview with a solution-oriented mindset. Be clear about how you plan to address the concerns raised and demonstrate your commitment to improvement. This will not only strengthen your relationship with employers or clients, but also show your professionalism.

Negotiating rates and contracts:

With the shift from side hustle to main hustle comes the need to rethink rates and contracts. Communicate transparently any changes to your pricing structure or terms. If you are raising rates, provide a clear rationale for the adjustment and emphasize the value you bring.

Negotiations should be conducted professionally and with a focus on mutual benefit. Clearly describe the deliverables and timelines associated with the new terms and ensure both parties are on the same page. Effective negotiation skills contribute to a successful transition and help maintain a positive relationship.

Building a personal brand:

As your side hustle evolves into your main hustle, your personal brand becomes more and more important. Consistent and authentic communication contributes to the development of your brand. Whether through social media, personal websites or other channels, communicate your passion, expertise and dedication to your work.

Engage your audience with thoughtfully crafted content. Share insights, showcase successes and highlight your commitment to delivering exceptional value. This not only attracts new opportunities, but also strengthens your reputation with existing employers or clients.

Transparent navigation in challenges:
The journey from the side hustle to the main hustle is not without problems. Transparency is key, whether you're facing unexpected obstacles or managing a larger workload. Communicate challenges proactively and outline your plan to address them.

This openness fosters trust and understanding. Employers and clients appreciate honesty and openness to challenges demonstrates your commitment to overcoming obstacles and delivering on your promises.

Communicating effectively with employers or clients while transitioning from side hustle to main hustle is a multifaceted process. It includes understanding your audience, setting clear expectations, providing regular updates, leveraging technology, managing feedback, negotiating terms, building your personal brand, and navigating challenges transparently.

By mastering these communication skills, individuals can not only ensure a smooth transition, but also cultivate strong, long-term relationships that contribute to the continued success of their main hustle.

5.4 Scaling Up and Scaling Down Strategies

Scaling and scaling strategies are key considerations for individuals transitioning from side hustle to main. As this journey unfolds, entrepreneurs often find themselves at the crossroads of growth, requiring careful planning and strategic decisions to meet future challenges.

Scaling: Unlocking the Potential

One of the key aspects of turning a side hustle into a main hustle involves expanding operations. It is essentially about expanding the scope, reach and impact of a business to meet the demands of a larger market. Successful scaling requires a multifaceted approach that begins with a thorough assessment of the existing business model.

1. Market Research and Analysis:

Before embarking on the journey of expansion, entrepreneurs must immerse themselves in comprehensive market research. Understanding industry trends, consumer behavior and potential competitors can provide valuable insights for fine-tuning products or services and identifying new opportunities.

2. Operational Efficiency: Streamlining operations is critical to scalability. Businesses should invest in technology and systems that increase efficiency, automate repetitive tasks and enable better use of resources. This not only increases productivity but also lays a solid foundation for growth.

3. Financial Management: Adequate financial planning is paramount in expansion. Entrepreneurs need to evaluate the capital required for expansion considering factors such as marketing,

infrastructure and personnel. Access to funding sources, including loans or investors, may be necessary to support this growth.

4. **Marketing and Branding:** A successful transition to mainstream often involves a more intensive marketing and branding strategy. Entrepreneurs must focus on building a strong brand identity, reaching a wider audience through targeted marketing campaigns and creating a compelling online presence.

5. Team Building: As the business expands, so does the need for a capable team. Hiring skilled professionals and fostering a collaborative work environment are essential components of scaling up. Entrepreneurs should invest time and resources in recruiting, training and retaining talented individuals who are aligned with the company's vision.

Reduction: Navigating Challenges

On the contrary, downsizing is a strategic approach that entrepreneurs may need to use when faced with challenges or changes in the business environment. This could include reducing traffic, optimizing costs or rethinking the overall business strategy.

1. Adaptability and Flexibility: Business is inherently dynamic and unpredictable challenges can arise. The ability to scale requires adaptability and flexibility. Entrepreneurs must be prepared to rethink their business model and make strategic decisions to weather economic downturns or unexpected disruptions.

2. Cost Optimization: Reduction often requires careful cost control. Entrepreneurs should identify areas where expenses can be reduced without compromising the quality of products or services. This may include renegotiating contracts, reducing unnecessary overhead, or implementing cost-effective alternatives.

3. Diversification: To mitigate the risks associated with curtailment, entrepreneurs can explore diversification strategies. This could include expanding product lines, entering new markets or taking advantage of complementary business opportunities that provide stability in challenging times.

4. Customer Retention: During a downsizing period, it becomes paramount to maintain a loyal customer base. Clear communication, transparency of changes and a focus on customer satisfaction can help retain existing clients. Providing value through loyalty programs or exclusive offers can strengthen customer relationships.

5. Strategic Partnerships: Working with strategic partners can be a viable approach to solving problems during the reduction phase. By establishing alliances with other businesses, entrepreneurs can gain access to shared resources, expertise, or alternative distribution channels that help sustain the business.

The decision to scale up or scale down is not binary; it requires a detailed understanding of the business environment and a good awareness of internal and external factors. Businesses must constantly evaluate key performance indicators, monitor market trends, and assess the overall health of the business in order to make informed decisions.

1. Data-Driven Decision Making: Leveraging data analytics is essential for entrepreneurs transitioning from side hustle to main hustle. Data-driven insights provide a solid foundation for decision-making, helping entrepreneurs identify patterns, predict market trends, and make strategic decisions that align with business goals.

2. Strategic Planning: A well-defined business strategy serves as a blueprint for an entrepreneur. Whether scaling up or down, the strategic plan should include short-term and long-term goals,

anticipated challenges, and contingency measures. Regularly reviewing and revising this plan ensures its relevance in an ever-changing business environment.

3. Continuous Learning: Entrepreneurship is a journey of continuous learning. Staying informed about industry developments, attending relevant workshops or conferences and networking with colleagues contributes to a holistic understanding of the business ecosystem. This knowledge enables entrepreneurs to make informed decisions at every stage of their journey.

Moving from side hustle to main hustle is a transformative journey that requires strategic thinking, adaptability, and resilience. Scale up and scale out strategies are indispensable tools in the entrepreneur's arsenal, providing the flexibility needed to navigate the complexities of the business environment. By carefully balancing growth initiatives with risk mitigation measures, entrepreneurs can chart a path to sustainable success in their core endeavors.

Conclusion

In conclusion, the journey from side hustle to main hustle is a dynamic and transformative process that reflects the evolving landscape of modern work. As individuals embark on this journey, they experience challenges, seize opportunities, and undergo personal and professional growth. The transition is not just about financial gains, but also a shift in mindset, resilience and adaptability. From the initial spark of a side project to the realization of a full-fledged main hustle, the journey is marked by strategic decision-making, dedication and a willingness to learn.

The rise of the gig economy has paved the way for more people to explore and capitalize on their skills and passions. The flexibility provided by side hustles allows individuals to experiment, test ideas, and gradually build a foundation for a sustainable main hustle. This iterative process often involves balancing the security of traditional employment with the uncertainty of entrepreneurship, requiring individuals to carefully evaluate their risk tolerance and long-term goals.

In addition, the integration of technology and the widespread use of online platforms have democratized access to markets and allowed side hustlers to reach a global audience. This shift has expanded opportunities for diverse talent and market niches, fostering a culture of creativity and innovation. As the side hustle gains momentum and attention, individuals must strategically position themselves in the market to stand out and attract potential customers.

Financial aspects play a key role in transitioning from a side hustle to a main one. Managing revenue streams, budgeting effectively and reinvesting profits are key parts of this process. The ability to scale a side hustle requires a strategic approach to resource allocation and a clear understanding of market dynamics. Individuals may encounter setbacks and uncertainties as they navigate the financial aspects of their business, but these challenges add to the learning curve and resilience needed for long-term success.

The emotional and psychological aspects of the journey are equally important. Balancing the demands of a side hustle with other life commitments can be challenging, requiring effective time management and prioritization. Moving into the mainstream often involves leaving the comfort zone of a stable job, which can be accompanied by fear and self-doubt. Overcoming these emotional obstacles is an integral part of the journey and individuals must develop a mindset that embraces change, learning and persistence.

Networking and mentoring play a vital role in this transformational process. Building a support system of like-minded individuals, mentors, and coworkers provides valuable insights, guidance, and emotional support. Learning from the experiences of others who have successfully transitioned from side hustles to majors can offer valuable lessons and shortcuts to speed up your own journey.

The social consequences of the side hustle phenomenon are also noteworthy. The traditional concept of a linear career path is evolving and more and more individuals are choosing different and non-linear trajectories. This shift challenges conventional notions of success and stability and highlights the importance of adaptability and continuous learning in a rapidly changing world. As the gig economy grows, policy makers and institutions must adapt to support this changing environment and ensure that individuals have the resources and protections necessary for sustainable and fulfilling careers.

Going from side hustle to main hustle is a multi-faceted and transformative experience that goes beyond financial gains. It involves a mix of strategic decision-making, financial management, emotional resilience and a commitment to lifelong learning. As individuals navigate this dynamic path, they contribute to an evolving work environment, reshape traditional notions of success, and take advantage of the opportunities offered by the gig economy. The side hustle phenomenon is not just a trend, but a reflection of a shifting paradigm in how individuals approach their careers and pursue their passions in the 21st century.

Long-term Benefits of Side Hustles to Main Hustle Transition

Moving from side hustle to main hustle is a significant and transformative journey that brings a variety of long-term benefits. This transition is not just a shift in professional life; it's a strategic move that can change your career path and financial stability. In this examination of the long-term benefits of transitioning from side hustle to main hustle, we'll dive into the key aspects that contribute to a successful transition and how it can impact an individual's life for years to come.

1. Financial stability and growth:

The most immediate and tangible benefit of moving from side hustle to main hustle is the potential for increased financial stability and growth. A main business usually provides a more consistent and substantial income compared to a side business, allowing individuals to better manage their spending, save and invest in their future. This increased financial stability lays the foundation for a secure and prosperous long-term financial journey.

2. Professional development:

A side hustle often serves as a testing ground for skills and ideas. The transition to the main hustle provides an opportunity for deeper professional development. With increased commitment and focus on the main hustle, individuals can hone their expertise, expand their skills, and become industry leaders. This continuous professional growth is beneficial not only for individuals, but also contributes to the overall development of the chosen field.

3. Job security and benefits:

Major issues often come with additional benefits such as job security, health benefits, retirement plans, and more. These elements contribute significantly to an individual's overall well-being and provide a safety net in the long run. Access to these benefits is a critical aspect of transitioning to the mainstream, as it provides a comprehensive support system that goes beyond monetary compensation.

4. More Networking Opportunities:

The main hustle often involves a larger network of colleagues, clients, and industry professionals. This expanded network opens the door to new opportunities, collaborations and partnerships. Over time, these connections can prove invaluable, offering insights, mentorship, and potential career paths. Networking is a long-term benefit that continues to pay off throughout your career.

5. Business growth and innovation:

For those transitioning from the side hustle with entrepreneurial aspirations, transitioning into the main hustle provides a platform for sustainable growth and innovation. Increased resources, both financial and human, enable the exploration of new ideas, expansion into untapped markets, and the establishment of a more robust business infrastructure. This entrepreneurial growth is a catalyst for long-term success and resilience in a dynamic business environment.

6. Improving work-life balance:

While switching to your main hustle may require more time and effort at first, it often leads to a better work-life balance in the long run. Main hustles, especially those associated with passion and expertise, tend to offer a more structured and predictable work environment. This balance contributes to overall well-being, reducing stress and burnout commonly associated with the unpredictability of side hustles.

7. Personal Branding and Recognition:

The main hustle provides a more prominent platform for personal branding and recognition. As individuals become more deeply embedded in their main hustle, their expertise and contributions are likely to gain wider recognition in their industry. This recognition not only boosts self-confidence, but also opens doors to other opportunities, including speaking, collaboration and leadership roles.

8. Older Building:

Moving from side hustle to main hustle allows individuals to build a lasting legacy in their chosen field. Whether through significant contributions, innovative projects or leadership roles, the main hustle provides the foundation for lasting impact. This legacy not only serves as a source of individual pride, but also inspires and influences future generations.

9. Diversification of income streams:

With the stability and growth that a main hustle offers, individuals can explore other sources of income. Diversification of income sources is a key strategy for long-term financial security, whether through investment, consulting or branching out into related businesses. This adaptability ensures resilience to economic changes and market fluctuations.

10. Improved Quality of Life:

Ultimately, moving from a side hustle to a main hustle contributes to an increased quality of life. The combination of financial stability, professional growth and a supportive work environment creates the foundation for a fulfilling and prosperous life. This positive impact extends beyond the professional sphere and affects personal relationships, health and overall well-being.

The long-term benefits of moving from side hustle to main hustle are multifaceted and impactful. From financial stability and professional development to better networking and work-life balance, this transition is a strategic move that shapes not only an individual's career, but their overall life journey. When individuals make this transition, they are positioned for lasting success and leaving a lasting legacy in their chosen field.

www.ingramcontent.com/pod-product-compliance
Lightning Source LLC
Chambersburg PA
CBHW071204290526
45796CB00008B/141